SIGN LANGUAGE LINK

A Pocket Dictionary
of Signs

CATH SMITH

Original drawings D. Hodgson
New additions C. Smith

CO-SIGN
COMMUNICATIONS

CO-SIGN COMMUNICATIONS

First published 1998
Revised edition 1999 (ISBN 0 9535069 0 8)
Third edition 2002 Reprinted 2003
ISBN 0 9535069 5 9

Published by Co-Sign Communications,
Stockton-on-Tees
Tel: 01642 580505 Fax: 01642 808959
email: cath@deafsign.com   www:deafsign.com

Distributed by Forest Bookshop Warehouse,
Unit 2 The New Building, Ellwood Road, Milkwall,
Coleford, Gloucestershire. GL16 7LE
Tel: 01594 833858 Fax: 01594 833446
email:Forest@forestbooks.com
www.ForestBooks.com

Printed in Great Britain by Alphabet Press,
17 Southview, Bear Park Durham, DH7 7DE Tel: 0191 3854868

By the same author

SIGNS MAKE SENSE: A Guide to British Sign Language
Souvenir Press

SIGN IN SIGHT: A Step into the Deaf World
Souvenir Press

SIGN LANGUAGE COMPANION:
A Handbook of British Signs
Souvenir Press

From Co-Sign Communications

SIGNS OF HEALTH:
A Pocket Medical Sign Language Guide

SIGN LANGUAGE LINK: Desk Edition

LET'S SIGN: BSL Building Blocks Tutor and CD-Rom

LET'S SIGN: BSL Building Blocks Student Primer

LET'S SIGN:
BSL Greetings Signs and Fingerspelling Wallchart (A2)

LET'S SIGN:
A4 Poster/Mats Set 1
Greetings-Family-Feelings-Questions

LET'S SIGN: A4 Bildtafeln zur Deutschen
Gebärdensprache
Tätigkeiten - Familie - Fragen - Gefühle

LET'S SIGN: Early Years

LET'S SIGN: For Work

Dedicated to

Peter Paul Quinn and Norah Quinn

in loving memory
and gratitude

ACKNOWLEDGEMENTS

My grateful thanks and appreciation go to;

My family, for their years of support and encouragement – my husband David, son William, sister Margaret, cousin Patricia, and Elsie and Ernest Smith my parents in-law.

To Beverley School for deaf children for permission to use these illustrations in my previous books SIGNS MAKE SENSE, SIGN IN SIGHT and SIGN LANGUAGE COMPANION, a selection of which are used again here in a completely new format.

To Dr. Terry Morris, head of the school from 1979 – 1994, for having the courage to stand alone in bringing sign language to an 'oral' school, for being among the first to appoint Deaf sign language users to his staff, and for his vision in setting up the Sign Dictionary Project, which made possible all of the books that followed. Myself and countless others have much to thank him for.

To my Deaf co-workers Anita Duffy, Malcolm Haywood, Pauline Hodgson, Craig Jones and Sandra Teasdale for their tolerance at continually being being pestered with 'how do you sign ----- ?' and their generosity in sharing their native expertise with all those willing to learn – many many thanks.

To Robert Riley and Stephen Smith of Alphabet Press, Stockton, for trusting me with their computer and keeping me constantly supplied with cups of tea. Their enthusiasm in the initial production of this book, and particularly their help with the detailed text revisions in the second and third editions is very much appreciated.

CONTENTS

British Sign Language, like all living languages, continues to evolve and change.

Sign Language Link was first published in 1998, and this third edition reflects some of its recent developments, with changes to detail and additions to the contents. The Useful Contacts section is fully revised, and the Left-handed Fingerspelling alphabet and Deafblind alphabet have been added.

The work to regularly update this book is ongoing, and feedback is always welcomed.

The world of the internet and electronic communications brings more access to information for hearing and Deaf people alike.

In January 2000, Co-Sign Communications along with web-designers INS and help from Tees Valley Training and Enterprise Council set up the interactive information site **www.deafsign.com** which was featured on Channel 4 Television in June 2000.

The site provides a useful resource and popular forum for information, news, interactive signing and fingerspelling games, questions, comments, with a section for schools and excellent links.

Please visit and join in.

INTRODUCTION

Sign languages exist the world over wherever groups of Deaf* people come together, but although they are different languages, they share structures based on visual/spatial grammars that enable Deaf people from different countries to quickly establish common ground and understand each other.

British Sign Language (BSL) is the language of Britain's Deaf community, and in spite of regional variation (similar to dialect and accent in spoken language) it is used and understood by Deaf people throughout England, Wales, Scotland and Northern Ireland. With its two-handed fingerspelling system, it is even found on the other side of the world in Australia and New Zealand where it forms the basis of Auslan (Australian Sign Language). Early childhood deafness, with its profound effects on language and communication, is a shared experience, and Deaf people whose dominant language is BSL and **not English** represent the majority of Deaf community members.

* The convention of the upper case 'D' in *Deaf* refers to people who identify themselves as culturally Deaf sign language users.

However, the situation for most Deaf individuals is unusual compared to other language minority groups. For example, language is usually passed on from one generation to the next within families in a local community of language users. This rarely happens with BSL. The incidence of infant deafness is roughly one child in every thousand randomly distributed across the country, with the majority (90%) born to families who know nothing of deafness and are not themselves sign language users, at least in the early stages after diagnosis.

In addition, BSL was believed to deter deaf children's development of spoken language and was actively discouraged by deaf educationalists for over 100 years, an attitude still endorsed by many hearing professionals in spite of strong opposition from Deaf people. Deaf children **need** access to fluent and natural sign language users both within their own peer group, and through contact with adult sign language users – the Deaf role models who understand what it is like to be a deaf child in a hearing world.

Deaf people themselves greatly value their language and community with the whole shared experience of growing up deaf giving a totally different perspective on life, even to the extent that deafness itself is rarely seen as a problem. This can bring about the shared feeling of belonging and sense of closeness that leads Deaf people to seek each other out, and which can make people who aren't Deaf feel like outsiders.

Deaf people also live and work in the hearing world, and need and value their skills in English too. From their birth into a hearing family, to the birth of their own hearing children (90% of children born to Deaf couples are hearing), contact with the hearing world is inescapable and is handled with competence and confidence based on a lifetime's experience. It is hearing people who might feel inadequate, or suffer from culture shock when they encounter the Deaf world, driving greater and greater numbers to learn more about sign language.

This pocket book of sign language vocabulary is designed to assist such people, by providing an easily accessible form of reference for the numerous everyday situations in which Deaf and hearing people interface. To fulfill the most constant requests from Deaf people, it is packed with as much information on context and variation as possible within this convenient format.

This gives a glimpse of the complexities of the language but the grammatical constructions of BSL require a visual way of thinking and of structuring thought that are outside the scope of a pocket dictionary (see SOURCES AND RECOMMENDED READING for further study). The best way to learn is through sign language classes and contact with Deaf people.

The signs contained within are the **building blocks** of the language, capable of being inflected, modified and combined to express all the ideas, feelings and opinions that spoken language gives to those who are not Deaf.   It is intended to give hearing people equal responsibility for successful communication – sharing ideas and information in a way that is neither patronising nor condescending, but which offers equality and respect.

Even for those who have not yet had contact with Deaf people, BSL is a language worthy of study in its own right – a testament to the human mind's ability, when denied access to spoken language, to fulfill its basic need and instinct for language construction – in an entirely different medium.

GUIDE TO HEADINGS AND CAPTIONS

Languages have very few direct word for word equivalents between each other, and the headings given for each sign are a guide to meaning rather than a direct translation.

Where possible, more than one word heading is given, to give a clearer idea of its context.

The captions are intended to give extra information on the handshape, location and movement of signs.

Details of non-manual features (**facial/bodily expressions**) **variation,** and changes in **context** are given in **bold text** when relevant and where space allows. Additional meanings are given in ***bold italics***.

Signs and fingerspelling are described and illustrated as if the signer is right-handed, with the right hand always referred to as R. and the left hand as L.

Left-handed signers will use the reverse of this, with the left hand as dominant.

From the thumb, the fingers are referred to as index, middle, ring and little finger.

DIRECTION, ORIENTATION
AND MOVEMENT

Terms used to describe the direction in which the hands face, point or move are given here. Description of hand orientation is based on the direction in which the palm faces regardless of whether the hand is open or closed.

As illustrated here, the R. hand is palm left and the L. hand is palm right, or they can also be described as palm facing, or palm in.

The hand may be described as '*pointing*' up, forward etc., even if the fingers are bent in a different direction or closed.

As illustrated, both hands are pointing forward, palms facing.

Diagonal movements are described '*forward/left*' or '*back/right*' and so on.

Some signs start with a full description of handshape and position before movement is made. This is then called a **formation**, which means they keep their position together as they move.

BASIC HANDSHAPES

Closed Hand

Flat Hand

Clawed Hand

Fist

Bent Hand

Bunched hand

'C' Hand

'M' Hand

Full 'C' Hand

Full 'O' Hand

'L' Hand

Irish T Hand

'N' Hand

'Y' Hand

'O' Hand

Open Hand

'V' Hand

These are frequently used handshapes in BSL and the terms used in this book to describe them. If the handshapes are described for example as **index, middle finger and thumb extended**, then it is understood that the other fingers are closed.

15

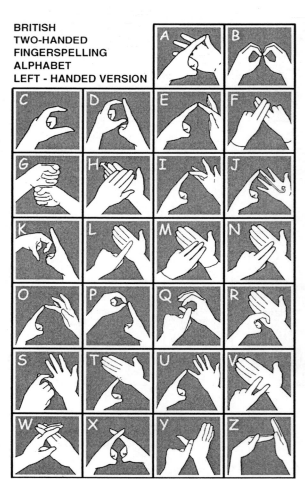

BRITISH
TWO-HANDED
FINGERSPELLING
ALPHABET
LEFT - HANDED VERSION

© 2002 Cath Smith   See 'About Finger Spelling' page 138.

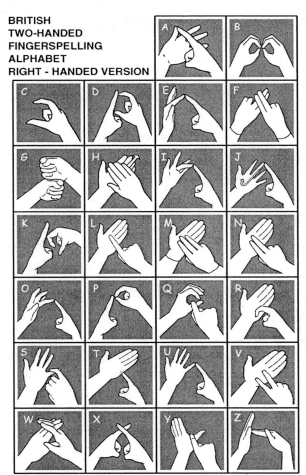

BRITISH TWO-HANDED FINGERSPELLING ALPHABET RIGHT - HANDED VERSION

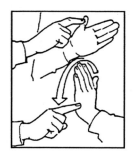

ABOUT, CONCERNING

Fingerspell 'A', then sweep R. index around L. fingertips to form 'T', or edge of R. fist with index extended, rubs in circles on L. palm. **May vary**.

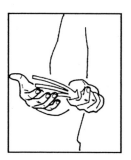

ACCEPT, GET, RECEIVE

Open hand held slightly forward, palm up, moves back towards body as it closes to a fist. **Both hands may be used**.

ACCESS, THROUGH

Fingers of R. flat hand move forward/left through fingers of L. hand. Also means *butt in*, *interfere*, *interrupt*. **May change direction in context**.

ACCIDENT

Fingerspell 'A', then form 'C' with R. hand in two small hops to the right, or R clawed hand shakes to and fro at side of head. **Shoulders lift. Will vary**.

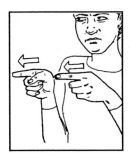

ACCUSE, BLAME

Index fingers point and move sharply forward, or in direction of person referred to. **The brows are furrowed and the eyes narrowed**.

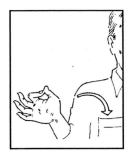

ADVANTAGE, PROFIT, GAIN

R. 'O' hand twists up and over from palm up to palm down, so that index and thumb tips brush down side of chest. Also means *benefit*.

AEROPLANE, FLY, FLIGHT

'Y' hand makes short movement forward/up at head height. May move down onto L. palm (***airport, landing***).

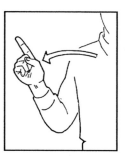

AFTER, LATER

Index finger pointing up twists to the right in small arc (may be repeated), or extended thumb twists from palm down to palm up (forward or right). **Varies**.

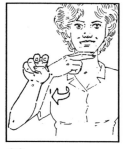

AFTERNOON

Fingertips of 'N' hand contact chin, then twist at the wrist to point forward, or brush forward against tips of L. 'N' hand (**regional**).

AGAIN, OFTEN, REPEAT

Palm left R. 'V' hand makes small repeated shaking movement forward/down. Also means *frequently*.

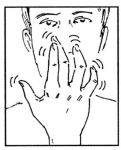

AGE, AGED, HOW OLD?

Open hand is held palm back in front of nose with fingers wiggling. **Raised or furrowed eyebrows** show question form, as in *how old? what age?* etc.

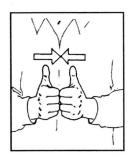

AGREE, APPOINTMENT

Closed hands with thumbs up move in to contact at the knuckles. **The head nods with lips pressed together**. Also means *appropriate*, *suitable*.

ALARM (e.g. fire), BELL

Edge of extended R. index finger bangs against L. palm several times. Also means *alarm clock*, *bell ring*.

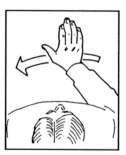

ALL, EVERYONE

Flat hand held with palm facing down, sweeps sideways in horizontal arc in front of body.

ALL RIGHT, FINE, OK

Closed hand/s with thumbs up and pointing slightly outwards, move in small outward circles (also a regional sign for *finished*). **Varies.**

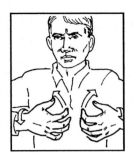

ANGRY, FRUSTRATED, MAD

Clawed hand/s move sharply up body, twisting to palm up (also **temper**), **brows furrowed**, **cheeks puffed**. Can be signed with alternate movements.

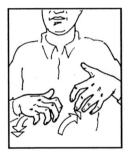

ANIMAL, CREATURE

Clawed hands, palms facing down, make repeated forward circular clawing movements alternately.

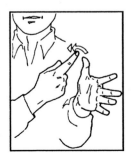

ANSWER, REPLY

Tip of extended R. index finger brushes backwards against tip of L. thumb several times. L. hand may be closed with thumb up.

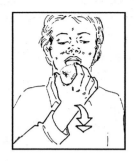

APPLE, FRUIT

Full 'C' hand, palm back in front of mouth, twists sharply to palm up twice. A single sharp movement may be used. **Handshape may vary slightly**.

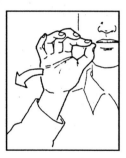

ASK, REQUEST

R. 'O' hand near side of mouth, moves forward in small arc, or palm forward bent hand makes short repeated forward movement. **Directional**.

ATTITUDE

Flat hand held palm back in front of face, moves forward, twisting to palm forward.

AWAKE, AWARE/NESS

Index fingers flick open off thumbs at sides of eyes. Eyes may briefly close, then open with movement (also *wake up*). One hand only may be used.

BABY, INFANT, DOLL

Arms rock from side to side in cradling movement. Sometimes signed with small up and down movements.

BAD, TERRIBLE, SERIOUS

Little finger held up makes small movement (forward, back or side to side). **Face and body indicate negative form.** Both hands can be used.

25

BANANA

Hands make action of holding and peeling a banana. Can be signed by thumbs and index fingers moving apart in outline shape.

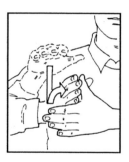

BECAUSE

L. flat hand held with thumb up. R. flat hand contacts edge of L. index, then inside of L. thumb. See also page 107, *reason*, *because*, *why?*

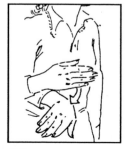

BEEN, DONE

Flat hand flips over in quick movement to palm down. Also means *from*, *where from?* **Raised eyebrows indicate question form**.

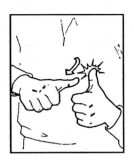

BEST

Tip of R. thumb strikes tip
of L. thumb in single
sharp movement
forward.

BETTER

Tip of R. thumb brushes
forward against tip of L.
thumb twice.

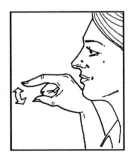

BIRD, BEAK

Thumb and index finger
open and close in front of
mouth several times.

BIRTHDAY

Edges of flat hands, palm up, on sides of waist, move forward/in (**birth**, **born**), then sweep upwards and apart, palm back. Regional. **Varies**.

BISCUIT

Fingertips of R. clawed hand tap left elbow twice. **May vary regionally**.

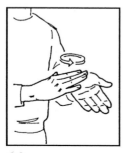

BLUE

Fingers of R. flat hand rub in small circles on L. palm or wrist. Can be made on back of palm down L. hand. **Colours vary regionally**.

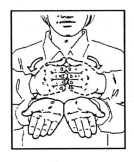

BOOK, CATALOGUE

Flat hands contact each other, palm to palm, then twist open to palm up in the action of a book opening. Movement may be repeated.

BOOK, BOOKING, RESERVE

Knuckles of closed hands tap together (also means *appointment*). Can be R. flat hand flipping over to palm down on L. palm, or other variation.

BORE/D, BORING, DULL

Fingers of flat hand tap chin several times in action of stifling a yawn, with **appropriate facial/bodily expression, and mouth slightly open**.

BOY

Extended R. index brushes left across chin. Can be index and thumb stroking down chin, or tips of 'N' hand brushing down chin. **Varies regionally**.

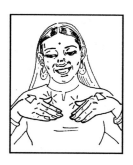

BREAK, REST, RELAX

Thumb tips of palm down hands move back to contact upper chest, **head may be tilted to one side**. Can be one hand only.

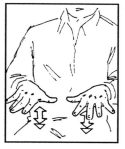

BRITAIN, BRITISH

Open hands, palm down, make small repeated downward movements, or palm back closed hands contact chest twice (**regional**).

BROTHER

Knuckles of two closed hands with thumbs up rub up and down against each other.

BUS, LORRY, VAN

Closed hands (can be palm up) move in steering action, or R. bent 'V' hand, palm left, moves slightly forward to give regional sign for **bus**.

CAKE, SCONE

Fingertips of R. clawed hand contact back of L. hand. Movement may be repeated.

CAN, ABLE, POSSIBLE

Palm back 'C' hand in front of nose moves forward/down as index flexes and **head nods**. Can be repeated. May start from the forehead.

CANCEL, CALL OFF

R. index draws a cross on palm of L. hand. Can be palm down flat hands which start crossed and move sharply apart.

CAN'T, UNABLE

Extended index moves down, looping over in the form of an X, as **the head shakes**. May start from forehead. Both hands can be used.

CAR PARK

The sign for *car* is followed by the sign *park* in which the edge of R. flat hand contacts L. palm several times, moving to the right.

CAREFUL, CAREFULLY

Index fingers held under eyes flex as hands move forward/down. **Eyes are open wide**. Also means *be careful*, *take care* and *expect* (**regional**).

CAT

Hands move out from sides of mouth as fingers flex, indicating whiskers. Can be R. hand stroking back of L. closed hand (**regional**).

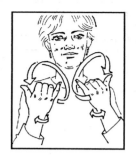

CELEBRATE, PARTY

'Y' hands rotate quickly at the wrists as hands move in towards each other, up, round and out again. **The cheeks are puffed**. Also means *have fun*, *social*.

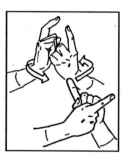

CHANGE, ALTER

Index fingers extended with hands facing and in contact, twist to change positions. Can be closed hands twisting against each other. **Varies**.

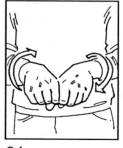

CHEAT, TWIST

Palm down fists twist against each other, **eyes narrowed**, or thumb tip moves down cheek (hand is closed, thumb out), also meaning *sly*, *crafty*.

CHECK, INSPECT, TEST

'Y' hands move down with quick alternate twisting movements from wrists. One hand may be used. **Directional**.

CHEEK/Y, INSULT, BARE

Bent index finger and thumb grasp cheek and make slight shaking movement.

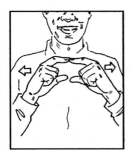

CHEQUE, NOTE, TICKET

Thumbs and index fingers move apart in outline shape, size may vary. 'Y' hands can be used, also moving apart in outline shape.

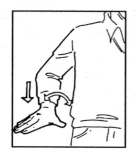

CHILDREN

Flat hand, palm down, makes small repeated downward movements a few inches apart (once for *child*). Two hands may be used, moving apart.

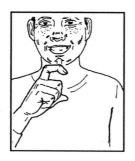

CHOCOLATE

Index edge of R. 'C' hand taps twice against the chin. Also one version of *jealous*. **Varies regionally**.

CHRISTMAS

Fingers of R. hand brush backwards across back of L. hand, then R. hand closes and moves down onto back of L. **One of several variations**.

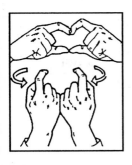

CLASS, CLASSROOM

Fingertips of 'C' hands touch, then hands swivel round in forward arc to finish with edges touching. **One of a number of variations**.

CLEAN, CLEAR

Fingers of R. flat hand sweep forward along palm of L. hand, or R. hand can be edge down on L. and sweep forward in repeated movement.

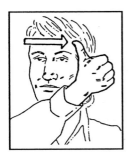

CLEVER, BRIGHT

Tip of extended thumb moves sharply across forehead, from right to left.

COACH

Full 'C' hands held facing each other, move sharply diagonally apart, R. backward/right and L. forward/left.

COFFEE

'C' hand near mouth makes small quick twisting movements   Can be edge of R. fist on top of L. fist making circular grinding movements.

COKE, COLA

'C' hand makes two short movements forward from side to side.

COLD, CHILLY, WINTER

Closed hands make short quick movements towards each other, elbows pulled into body in shivering action. **The cheeks are puffed**.

COLLEGE

'C' hand makes small quick twisting movements at side of the forehead. **One of several regional signs**.

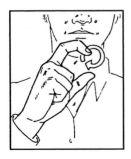

COLOUR

Palm left R. 'C' hand moves in small circles near chin, or palm forward open hand makes small vertical circles, or **other regional variations**.

COME, COME BACK

Upright index finger moves back towards body (finger may be bent). Index finger flexes several times for *come here*. **Directional**.

COMMUNICATE

'C' hands move backwards and forwards alternately. Full 'C' hands or palm up flat hands may also be used.

COMPLAIN, GRUMBLE

Fingertips of clawed hand brush upwards twice on chest. **Face and body indicate appropriate negative expression**.

COMPUTER

'C' hands make small simultaneous vertical circles, or fingers of palm down open hands wiggle, also meaning *keyboard*, *key in, type*.

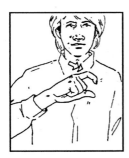

CONFIDENT

Index edge of R. 'C' hand taps chest twice. An upward movement means *gain confidence*, or downward means *lose confidence*.

CONTACT, JOIN, LINK

Both hands move towards each other and fingers of 'O' hands interlock. **Directional**. Also means *connect*, *connection*, and similar meanings.

41

CONTINUE, CARRY ON, STILL

Two 'C' hands move to the right, or move forward (may repeat). Can be one hand only. Short movement down gives *stay*, *remain*, *be still*.

COURSE, SCHEME

Thumb edge of R. 'C' hand moves down along left forearm, or along extended L. index finger.

DAILY, EVERY DAY

Backs of the fingers are brushed forwards across the cheek. Can be index finger tapping side of chin several times (**regional**).

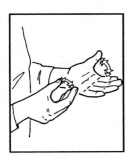

DAMP, MOIST, WET

The fingers are held straight as they open and close onto the thumbs several times.   One hand may be used.

DANCE, DANCING

Two 'V' hands make downward flicking movements from wrists as hands move from side to side. 'N' hands may be used, or **other variation**.

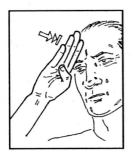

DANGER, DANGEROUS

Index edge of R. flat hand, palm left, moves sharply up to contact forehead.   May be repeated. Also means *risk*, *risky*.

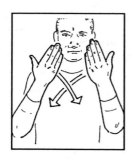

DARK, EVENING, NIGHT

Palm back flat hands swing in/down in front of face to cross each other. One of a number of variations for *evening*, *night*.

DATE, ADDRESS, LIVE

Closed hand taps side of chin twice, or front of chin (also *maths*, *number*), or can be signed with all the fingers upright and wiggling. **Regional**.

DAUGHTER, DAD, DADDY

Hands make quick repeated fingerspelt initial 'D'.

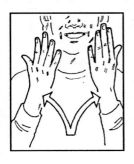

DAY, LIGHT

Flat hands held palm back in front of face, start crossed and swing upwards and apart from the elbows. *Day* is also often **fingerspelt**.

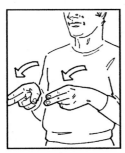

DEAD, DEATH, DIE

'N' hands, palm facing, twist sharply down from wrists to point forward. If movement is slow, the meaning is *dying*.

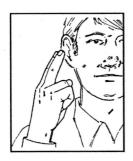

DEAF, DEAF PERSON

Extended fingers of 'N' hand contact ear. Cheeks may be puffed, meaning *profoundly deaf*, *really deaf*.

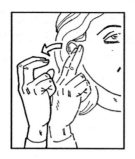

DEAF CLUB

Fingers of 'N' hand touch ear, then hand moves out slightly as fingers bend into 'C' shape. **Regional**. *Club* is often a **fingerspelt contraction**.

DIFFERENT

Extended index fingers held together, palm down, twist to palm up as hands move apart.

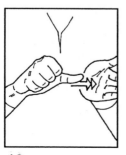

DIFFICULT/Y, PROBLEM

Tip of R. thumb taps centre of L. palm twice. Also means *hard*. **Cheeks may be puffed to show intensity**.

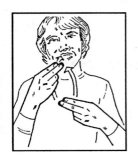

DINNER, MEAL

Palm back 'N' hands move up and down to mouth alternately. Can be two 'N' hands edge to edge making small sawing movement.

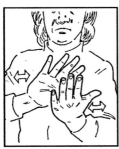

DIRTY, FILTHY, MUCKY

Open hands rub palms against each other, side to side, or in circular movement, with **negative facial expression**. **May vary**.

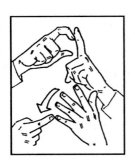

DISABLED, DISABILITY

Fingerspell 'D', then move R. index finger down along fingertips of L. open hand. **One of several variations**.

DISAGREE, DON'T AGREE

Closed hands, thumbs up, come together (*agree*), then spring open and apart as **the head shakes, lips pressed together, and brows furrowed**.

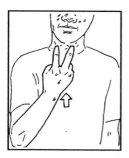

DISAPPOINT/ED

Fingertips of 'V' hand prod into neck. **The lips are pressed together, shoulders droop slightly**. Also a **regional** sign for *miss*.

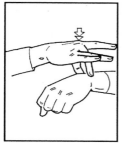

DOCTOR, MEDICAL

Tip of R. middle finger (or index) and thumb tap L. wrist twice, or 'O' hand moves side to side on chest (also *clinic*). **GP is usually fingerspelt**.

DOG

Fingers of 'N' hands held in "begging" position with small movements, or back of bent hand taps under chin, or flat hand taps thigh. **Regional**.

DON'T KNOW

Fingertips of flat hand touch forehead, then hand drops forward/down as the **head shakes and shoulders shrug**.

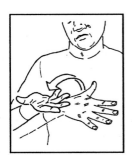

DON'T LIKE, DISLIKE

Open hand on chest twists to palm up (or down) pushing away emphatically with **negative expression and head shake**.

DON'T UNDERSTAND

Both index fingers flick backwards at sides of head, with lip-pattern 'Pow!' or 'Whoosh!' **Regional**. Also means *over my head*.

DRINK, GLASS

Full 'C' hand moves up towards mouth with small tipping movement.

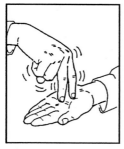

DRUNK, TIPSY

Fingers of R. 'V' hand (**legs classifier**) stand on L. palm, and bend as hand rotates slightly, or upright index makes small circles near head. **Varies**.

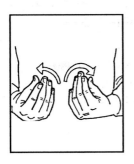

DRY, DRIED OUT

Thumbtips rub across the pads of the fingers (can be one hand). If hands also move apart can mean *solve*, *dissolve* and similar meanings.

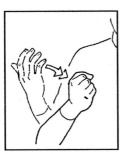

EARN, BENEFIT, INCOME

Palm up clawed hand moves in/down to body twice, closing to a fist. Also used for *dole*, *pension*, *wage* and other forms of income.

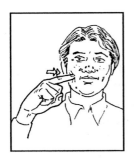

EASY, SIMPLE, SOFT

Tip of index finger prods twice into cheek. Cheeks may be puffed to show intensity, as in *dead easy*, *doddle*, for example.

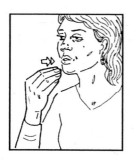

EAT, FOOD, SNACK

Bunched hand makes small repeated movement backwards towards mouth.

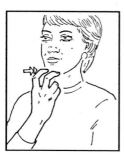

ELECTRIC/ITY, BATTERY

Fingertips of bent 'V' hand tap chin twice. Can also be signed with upright index moving sharply down in a zig-zag (*electricity*, *lightening*).

E-MAIL

Index (or middle) fingers make small flicking movements towards each other. One hand only may be used. **Directional**.

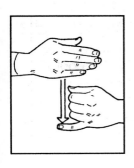

END, FINAL, LAST

Little finger edge of R. flat hand chops down onto extended L. little finger. R. hand may alternatively be palm down or palm up.

ENGLAND, ENGLISH

R. extended index finger makes small repeated rubbing movement forward/back along L. extended index finger.

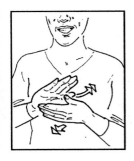

ENJOY, HAPPY, PLEASURE

Flat hands brush against each other repeatedly with **positive facial expression**, or flat hand rubs in circles on chest (*pleased*).

ENOUGH, PLENTY, AMPLE

Backs of fingers of palm back bent hand contact underside of chin in repeated brushing movement, forward/up. Also means *adequate*.

EQUIPMENT, MACHINE

Palm back clawed hands swivel towards each other from wrists so that fingers interlock. Also means *engineering*, *technology*.

EUROPE, EUROPEAN

Hand forms one-handed fingerspelling letter 'E' and makes small circular movement. Fingers may spring open several times (stars on the flag).

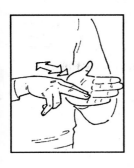

EXAM, TEST

Index edge of palm down R. 'N' hand rubs back and forth on L. palm, or closed hands crossed at wrists reverse places, or **other variations**.

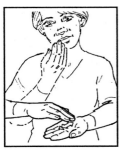

EXCUSE, PARDON ME

R. hand touches mouth, then rubs to and fro on L. palm (circular rubbing means *apologise*, *forgive*). Fingerspelt 'EX' also used.

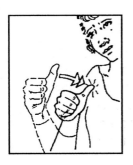

EXPECT, GOING TO, INTEND

Back of extended thumb taps side of upper chest twice. **The lips may be stretched as body moves forward slightly**.

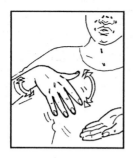

EXPENSIVE, DEAR

Tips of R. open hand tap L. palm, then R. hand moves to the right shaking from wrist. **Cheeks puffed to show intensity**, as in *extortionate*.

EXPERIENCE/D

Tip of extended R. thumb contacts forehead, then changes to flat hand brushing down across L. palm. **May vary**.

EXPLAIN, TELL ABOUT

Extended index moves from mouth, then flat hands rotate round each other, forward or back depending on **context**. Also means *relate*, *story*.

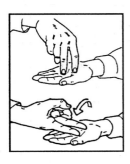

FALL, FALL OVER

Fingers of R. 'V' hand (**legs classifier**) stand on L. palm then twist over and land palm up on L. palm. Handshape and movement may change in context.

FAMILY

Hands form fingerspelt 'F' formation and make small horizontal circle. Can be palm down open hand in same movement.

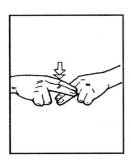

FATHER, DAD, DADDY

Extended fingers of fingerspelt 'F' tap together twice (also *Friday*, in some regions). Repeated initial 'D' also used for *dad, daddy, daughter*.

57

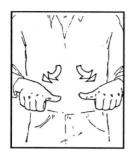

FAVOURITE, PREFERRED

Palm down closed hands with thumbs extended make two small downward movements. Also means *prefer*, *preference*. One of **several variations**.

FED UP, HAD ENOUGH

Backs of fingers of bent hand firmly contact underside of chin. **Face and body show negative feeling,** or can change meaning to *full*, *I'm full*.

FEEL, EMOTION, SENSE

Middle fingertips brush upwards on body (open hands may also be used). May be repeated. One hand may be used.

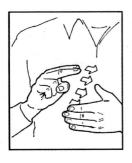

FILL IN (form), NOTE DOWN

R. 'N' hand makes several short forward movements as it moves down behind palm back L. flat hand. R. bent 'V' hand may alternatively be used.

FINGERSPELL, SPELL

Finger and thumb tips of bunched hands wiggle against each other as formation moves to the right (for British two-handed system).

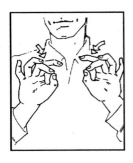

FINISH, COMPLETE

Middle fingers close repeatedly onto thumbs in quick repeated contact (**regional**). One hand may be used. **One of several variations**.

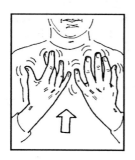

FIRE, BURN, FLAMES

Palm back hands move upwards with fingers wiggling. Hands can be palm facing, moving alternately up and down. **May vary in context**.

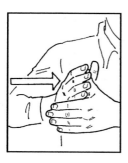

FIRST, INITIAL

Fingers of R. flat hand strike inside of L. thumb. Can be palm forward index twisting sharply to palm back, or **other regional variations**.

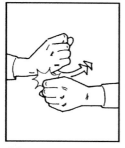

FIX, MEND, REPAIR

Edge of R. fist brushes across top of L. fist twice. Can also be signed with tips of bunched hands twisting against each other several times.

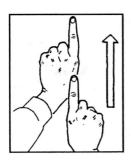

FOLLOW, GO ALONG WITH

Index fingers point and move forward R. behind L. Fingers may be held upright, (as **person classifiers**), as in *walk behind*, *shadow*, *stalk*.

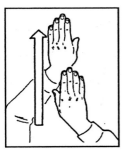

FOLLOW, TAIL, TAIL-GATE

Palm down flat hands used as vehicle classifiers move forward, R. behind L. Movement, location and direction **may change to suit context**.

FORGET, FORGETFUL

Fingertips of full 'O' hand touch side of forehead then hand springs open in short forward movement. **One of several variations**.

FREE, GRATIS, BLANK

R. hand of fingerspelt 'F' brushes forward twice along fingers of L. A circular movement gives a regional sign for *Friday*. **May vary**.

FRIEND, MATE, PAL

Hands clasp each other in short shaking movement, or closed hands, thumbs up, bang together or twist against each other (**regional**).

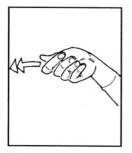

FRY, FRY UP, COOK, PAN

Thumb tucked into bent index; hand shakes backwards and forwards several times. Can be palm in 'V' hands twisting from the wrists.

FUNNY, ODD, STRANGE

R. index flicks out sharply across chin (also *weird*, *peculiar*) or middle fingertip flicks off thumb twice, or other **variation**. **The nose is wrinkled**.

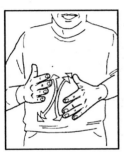

GAME, PLAY ABOUT

Open hands brush up and down alternately against each other several times. Can be repeated fingerspelt initial 'G', or **other variation**.

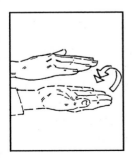

GARDEN/ING, DIG

Flat hand flips over from palm up to palm down in small repeated forward movement. **One of several variations**.

GIRL, LASS

Edge of index finger brushes forwards twice on cheek (or across chin). Can be index pointing left, moving to the right across the brow (**regional**).

GIVE, HAND OVER, LET

Palm up hands (or just one hand) move forward. **Direction or handshape may change to suit item in context**. Also means *gift*, *offer*, *pass*, *present*.

GO, GO AWAY, SEND

Index finger swings to point forward, away from the body. A flat hand can be used. **May change to suit context**.

GOD, BOSS, CHIEF, HEAD

Index finger held upright above head, moves forward slightly with stress, or can be small upward twist from wrist. Both hands for *authority*.

GOOD, GREAT, HELLO

Extended thumb makes small forward movement, both hands may be used for emphasis. **Raised eyebrows for question form**, as in *all right? ok?*

GOODBYE, BYE, CHEERIO

Fingers bend up and down several times, bending at palm knuckles in short movement, or hand waves slightly from side to side.

GOOD LUCK, LUCK, LUCKY

Index finger and thumb extended; tip of thumb brushes tip of nose as hand twists sharply forward to palm down. **One of several variations**.

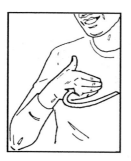

GOOD-MORNING, MORNING

Tips of R. bent hand, thumb up, contact left, then right upper chest. Can be two bent hands, or closed hands, moving up chest (**regional**).

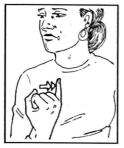

GUILT, GUILTY, MY FAULT

Edge of extended little finger taps chest twice. A circular movement gives a regional sign for *sorry*, *apologise*. **The lips may be pressed together**.

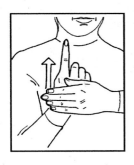

HAPPEN, CROP UP, OCCUR

R. index finger moves sharply up behind L. hand, or index finger flicks upwards in front of L. hand (emphatically for *sudden*, *suddenly*).

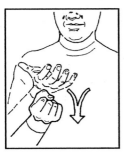

HAVE, GOT, POSSESS

Slightly clawed hand, palm up, makes small movement down, as it snaps shut, closing sharply to a fist.

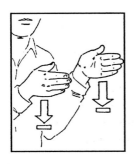

HAVE TO, INSIST, MUST

Palm facing flat hands held slightly apart, move down simultaneously with emphasis. Also means *compulsory*, *mandatory*, *obliged to*.

67

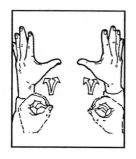

HEADLIGHTS, HEADLAMPS

Full 'O' hands make slight forward movement as they spring open. Repeated movement gives *flashing headlights*. **May change direction to suit context**.

HEARING, HEARING PERSON

Tip of extended index touches ear then chin (may tap twice on chin), or same movement with tip of extended thumb is sometimes used.

HEARING LOSS, DEAFENED

Fingers and thumb of bent hand close together as hand moves slightly down near ear. Slow movement indicates *gradual hearing loss*.

HELLO, HI

Palm forward open hand moves to the right in a small arc. May finish by closing to a fist with the thumb up, or **other variation**.

HELP, ASSIST/ANCE

R. closed hand rests on L. palm and formation moves forward or back, or in direction appropriate to context (**directional**).

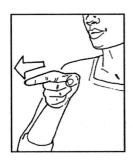

HER, HE, HIM, IT, SHE

Index finger points to indicate person or item referred to, accompanied by eye gaze. A sideways sweep indicates plural, eg *them*, *they*. **Directional**.

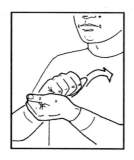

HIRE, BORROW, LEND

Closed hands crossed, one on top of the other, move back to body in a small arc (or move forward, depending on **context**). **Directional**.

HOPE, WISH

Crossed fingers move forward slightly (one hand only may be used) or palm left R. full 'C' closes sharply near mouth (**regional**).

HOSPITAL, FIRST AID

Tip of extended R. thumb (or index fingertip) draws small cross on left upper arm. **One of many variations**. Also means *ambulance*, *nurse*.

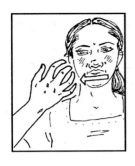

HOT, HEAT, HEATING

R. clawed hand is drawn sharply across the mouth, from left to right, or flat hand brushes across forehead, then shakes downwards (*phew*).

HOTEL, LODGE, STAY OVER

Flat hands (or hand) on sides of head, move down, twisting to palm down. Also means *accommodation*, *resident*, *residential*.

HOUSE, HOME

Extended fingers of 'N' hands contact at an angle, then move apart/down in outline shape of building. Flat hands may also be used.

HOW?

Knuckles of clawed hands tap together twice. The hands may be palm back or palm up. **The face and body indicate question form**.

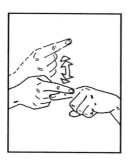

HURRY UP, QUICK/LY

Extended R. index taps on L. several times very quickly (a single sharp movement for *early*). Also means *emergency*, *fast*, *immediate*, *urgent*.

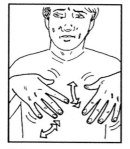

HURT, PAINFUL, SORE

Open hand/s shake loosely up and down alternately. Also means *injure*, *suffer*. **Face and body show pained expression**.

HUSBAND, WIFE, SPOUSE

R. index finger and thumb (or middle finger and thumb) make repeated contact with upper L. ring finger. Also means *wedding*, *ring*.

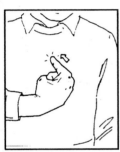

I, ME

Tip of extended index finger contacts the front of the chest.

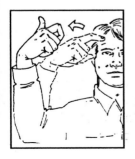

IDEA, NOTION

Index finger touches forehead, then moves out and bends with thumb up, or index flexed on thumb flicks up off forehead (also *understand*).

IGNORE, TAKE NO NOTICE

Extended index fingers (can be one hand only), flick down/sideways sharply from near ears. **May change direction in context**.

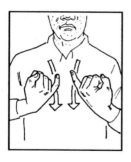

ILL/NESS, SICK, TIRED

Edges of little fingers brush downwards on chest (can be one hand only), or R. index touches forehead, then moves down to tap L. index.

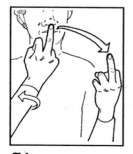

IMITATION, FAKE, MOCK

R. middle fingertip touches nose, twists and moves forward, then taps the L. middle fingertip twice. Also means *false*, *phoney*, *pretend*.

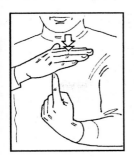

IMPORTANT, TOP

Palm of R. hand moves down to contact tip of L. index (may tap twice). R. hand may spring open from full 'O' hand as it comes down onto L. index.

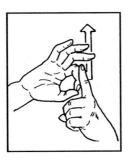

IMPROVE, IMPROVEMENT

Tips of index and thumb of R. 'O' hand move upwards along upright L. extended index finger.

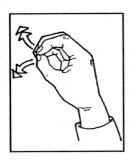

INDICATOR (vehicle)

Fingers of full 'O' hand spring open in small repeated movements. Direction of movement **will vary according to context**.

INTERNET, WEB

Open hands start with middle finger tips touching, then hands move down and round in sphere shape. **May vary slightly**.

INTERPRET, INTERPRETER

'V' hands make several small, quick alternate twisting movements backwards/forward from wrists. 'N' hands are also sometimes used.

INTERRUPT, INTERFERE

Fingers of R. hand prod through fingers of L. hand twice. Also means *butt in*. **Directional**. Single forward movement for *access*.

JOKE, HAVE ON, KID

Thumb tip of 'V' hand brushes twice across end of nose, or R. 'V' hand (or open hand) palm down, brushes forward twice along L. extended index.

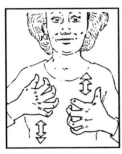

KEEN, EAGER, EXCITED

Tips of clawed hands rub alternately up and down chest **animatedly**. Also means *enthusiastic*, *interest/ed*, *motivated*, *stimulated*.

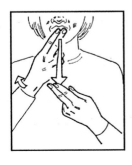

KISS, PECK

Tips of R. 'N' hand contact the lips, then twist to palm down and touch tips of L. 'N' hand. **May change in context. One of several variations**.

77

KITCHEN

Middle knuckle of bent R. extended index finger taps middle of L. extended index finger twice (repeated fingerspelt initial 'K').

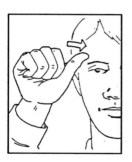

KNOW, KNOWLEDGE

Tip of extended R. thumb contacts side of forehead. Contact may be repeated. A forward flick of the thumb gives a regional sign for **understand**.

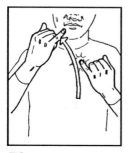

LAST, WORST

End of R. little finger hits tip of L. in upward (or downward) movement. Can be R. flat hand brought down onto L. little finger (**last**, **end**).

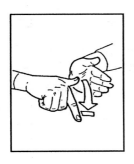

LATE, OVERDUE

R. thumb tip stays in contact with L. palm, as index pivots sharply forward/down. Can be index only, with thumb tucked in.

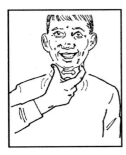

LAUGH, FUN, FUNNY

Bent index finger and thumb make small side to side shaking movements near chin. Two hands can be used in small alternate movement, L. under R.

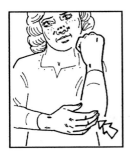

LAZY, IDLE

R. hand taps left elbow twice (R. clawed hand for *biscuit*), or palm back closed hands, with middle fingers up, move down twice.

LEARN, TAKE IN, STUDY

Open hand moves back to head as fingers close onto thumb. Index edges of palm down flat hands rub together for *learn*, *train*, *student*, *practice*.

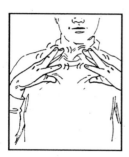

LEISURE, SPARE TIME

Thumb tips rest on chest as all the fingers wiggle (can be one hand only). **Head tilts to one side.** Also means *break*, *holiday*, *relax/ation*.

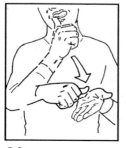

LETTER, MAIL

Tip of R. extended thumb touches mouth, then moves down to touch L. palm. In some regions also means *stamp*, *insurance*.

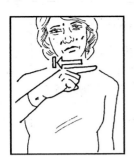

LIE, LIAR, FIB, UNTRUTH

Edge of R. extended index finger, pointing left, is drawn sharply left to right, across the chin. Is also one version of *Russia*, *Russian*.

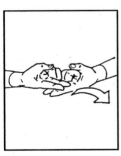

LIFT, RIDE, TRANSPORT

Extended fingers of R. 'N' hand lay across fingers of L. 'N' hand, palm up, as both hands move forward, meaning *give a lift/ride to*, *transport* in a car etc.

LIGHT- FLASHING DOORBELL

Thumb pushes slightly forward (*bell press*), then hand moves up as fingers spring open (*flashing-light*). This is an **alerting device** used by deaf people.

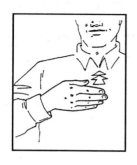

LIKE, FOND OF, ENJOY

Flat hand taps chest twice (also *front*). Open hand on chest moves forward, closing with index up to give *if you like*, *please yourself*.

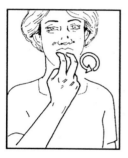

LIPREAD, LIPSPEAK/ER

Extended fingers of bent 'V' hand move in small circles near mouth. Also means *lip-pattern*, *oral*. **Directional** (can be palm forward, held forward).

LIVE, ADDRESS, ALIVE

Tip of middle finger on chest, rubs up and down several times. A clawed hand may be used. Also means *life* and is a regional sign for *toilet*.

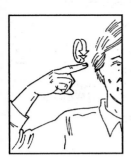

LONDON, NOISY, SOUND

Index finger points in and makes forward circles near ear, or palm down bent hands, move down slightly twice for *London, shopping* (**regional**).

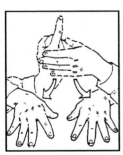

LONELY, ISOLATED

R. index moves down behind L. hand then both hands open and swing to point down. First part of sign also means *alone*, *individual*, *only*.

LOOK, SEE, WATCH

'V' hand moves forward from near eye, or can be located and/or moved in direction to suit the context (**fingers represent direction of eye gaze**).

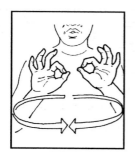

LOOP SYSTEM

'O' hands move forward, apart and round in an arc. Sign can be made on the body to refer to personal loop worn round the neck. This is a **listening device** for hearing aid users.

LOSE, LOST, DROP

Full 'O' hands move slightly down and apart as they spring open, palm down. The same movement, but palm up means *waste*, *wasted*.

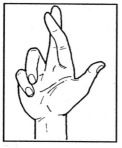

LOTTERY (National Lottery)

The hand is held with palm facing forwards, with the index and middle fingers crossed and thumb extended.

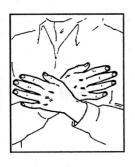

LOVE, AFFECTION

Hands are held crossed over on the chest. For *love, adore, fond of*, flat hands touch chest, then close with thumbs out and move forward, palm down.

MAKE, CREATE, FIX

Fingertips of bunched hands twist against each other twice (if hands also move up, the meaning is *construct*). Can be R. fist striking top of L. fist twice.

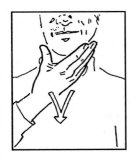

MAN, MALE, MASCULINE

Fingers and thumb stroke chin as fingers close onto thumb (can repeat), or palm left R. full 'C' hand moves forward from chin closing to a fist.

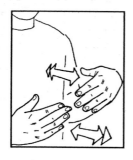

MANAGE, ARRANGE, SORT OUT

Fingers brush alternately forward and back against each other several times. In different contexts, can also mean *anyway*, *organise*, *never mind*.

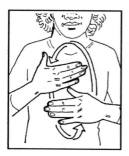

MANNER/S, BEHAVIOUR

Flat hands brush backwards down body alternately. With **head tilted** and **lips pressed together**, means *calm*, *patient*, *tolerant*.

MANY, LOTS, HOW MANY?

All the fingers wiggle as hands move apart (cheeks may be puffed). Also means *too many*, *too much*. **Raised eyebrows for question form**.

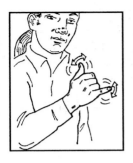

MAYBE, MIGHT, PERHAPS

'Y' hand makes quick twisting movements from the wrist (also **possibly**) or palm up flat hands move alternately up and down (also **doubt**, **uncertain**). **Lips may be stretched**.

MEAN/ING, STORY

Fingers of R. flat hand rub in small circles on palm of L. hand. Also means **context**, **explain**, **explanation**.

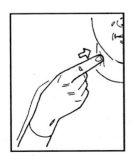

MEAT, BEEF, BUTCHER

Index fingertip prods into side of neck (may repeat), or bent index and thumb grasp cheek (also meaning **bare**, **flesh**, **insult**). As shown, also means **kill**.

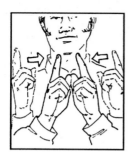

MEET, FACE TO FACE

Upright index fingers (person classifiers) move towards each other in **direction to suit context**. Without movement, meaning is *one to one*.

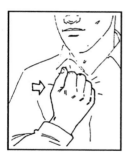

MINE, MY, BELONG TO ME

Closed hand firmly moves back onto chest.   Contact may be repeated.   Also means *belonging to me*, *my own*.

MINICOM, TEXT 'PHONE

Palm down L. 'Y' hand above wiggling fingers of palm down R. hand; move forward or back for *call by minicom*.

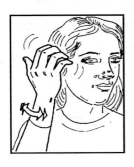

MISTAKE, ACCIDENT, SORRY

Clawed hand shakes slightly forward/back at side of head, or side to side in front of head or chin (palm back), or **other variation. Shoulders lift**.

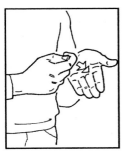

MONEY, CASH, FINANCE

R. hand, with thumb tucked into bent index, taps twice onto L. palm. **R. handshape may vary**, e.g. thumb of full 'C' hand on L. palm (*funds*).

MORE

R. palm back flat hand taps back of L. twice (L. hand may be closed), or hands start in contact, then R. moves forward (also meaning *further*, *onward*.

89

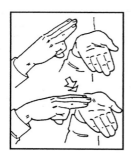

MOTHER, MUM, MUMMY

Extended fingers of R. 'M' hand tap L. palm twice. In some regions, 'M' hand taps side of forehead, or R. index taps back of L. ring finger twice.

NAME, CALL, CALLED

'N' hand touches side of forehead, then moves and twists forward, or palm facing 'V' hands move slightly outwards as fingers flex (*called*, *entitled*).

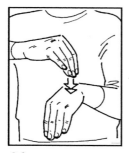

NAUGHTY, TROUBLE

Fingertips of R. bent hand tap back of L. hand (or forearm) twice. Also means *bother*, *nuisance*. **One of several variations**.

NEIGHBOUR, NEXT

Thumb extended from closed hand, twists from palm down to palm up. **Directional** (can be a forward movement, or other in **context**).

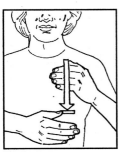

NEVER

Both hands held with palms facing back, R. flat hand brushes sharply down the back of L. hand (L. hand may be closed or bent). **The head shakes**.

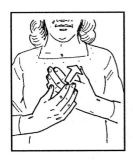

NEW, FASHION, MODERN

R. flat hand brushes up the back (or front) of the L. flat hand. May repeat. Also means *fresh* (the fingers of R. hand may open).

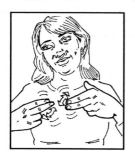

NEWS

Fingertips of 'N' hands brush backwards and forwards alternately against each other several times.

NICE, LOVELY, SWEET

Tip of thumb is drawn across chin (also *tasty*, *delicious*), or index of R. 'L' hand on cheek moves right and bends (also means *lovely, pretty*).

NO, DENY, REFUSE

Closed hand twists sharply from palm back to palm forward, as **the head shakes**. Can also mean *turn away* (**the head turns sharply**).

NOISE, LOUD, SOUND

Extended index finger, pointing inwards near ear, moves in forward circular movements.   Also one variation of **London**.

NORTHERN IRELAND, IRISH

Fingertips of R. bent 'V' hand tap back of L. closed hand twice. Also one version of **potato**.

NOT SURE, HESITANT

R. flat hand rests edge down on L. palm and wavers slightly side to side (**lips pressed together**). Also means **doubtful**, **uncertain**, **unsure**.

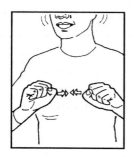

NOT YET, BEFORE

Two closed hands, palm forward/down, make small quick shaking movements, side to side, or up and down (also meaning *wait*, *hang on*). **Head shakes**.

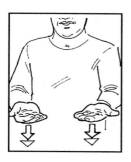

NOW, PRESENT, TODAY

Flat hands, palm up, make short repeated movement down. One sharp movement for *at once*, *right now*, *immediately*.

NURSERY

Extended middle finger tip taps the chin twice (**regional**). **One of several variations**.

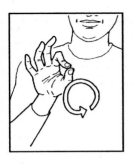

OFFICE

'O' hand, palm forward, moves in small circles (**regional**), or moves right, palm down, with small writing movements, or other variation.

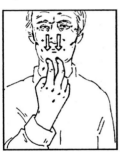

OLD, AGED, ELDERLY

'V' hand (or bent 'V' hand), palm back in front of nose, moves down as fingers flex, or hand bends backwards. Also **regional** for *dark*, *night*.

ORANGE

Clawed hand, palm forward (or palm left), opens and closes at side of mouth, or fingers may flex. Refers to the colour, fruit or drink.

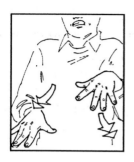

PANIC, FRANTIC

Open hands move repeatedly forward/down alternately. **The head twists from side to side with mouth slightly open.** Also means *apprehension*.

PARENT, PARENTS

Fingerspelt initial 'M' followed by fingerspelt initial 'F'. Also means *mother and father*, *mum and dad*.

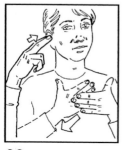

PARTIALLY DEAF

Edge of R. flat hand is drawn back/right across L. palm, (also means *half*, *part*) followed by tips of 'N' hand contacting ear (*deaf*).

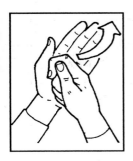

PAY, PAYMENT

R. hand moves forward off L. palm (**directional**). Repeated for *regular payment*, *rent*. R. h/shape may vary e.g. 'O' hand, full 'C', or bunched hand.

PEOPLE, HUMANITY

Thumb and index stroke chin, then index turns and brushes forward on cheek, or moves sharply down in front of body in zig-zag, or other **variations**.

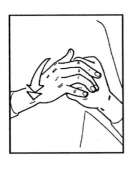

PET, CAT, STROKE

R. hand makes short repeated stroking movements down the back of L. closed hand. **Regional**.

PICK, CHOOSE, SELECT

Index finger closes onto thumb in short movement up/back.   Both hands may be used in alternate movements, also meaning *raffle*. **Directional**.

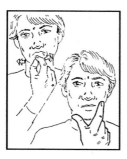

PILL, TABLET

Index finger and thumb flick open near mouth. May be repeated. R. hand may start in contact with L. palm before moving to mouth.

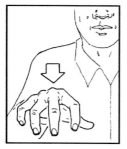

PLACE, TOWN, COUNTRY

Palm down clawed hand moves down slightly (can be above upright L. index).   May make small circular movement (open hand may also be used).

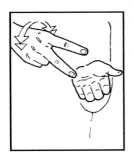

PLAN, DESIGN, STRATEGY

Fingertips of R. 'V' hand touch L. palm, as R. hand twists from palm back to palm down. Located on forehead means *translate*, *work out*, *change of mind*.

PLAY, GAME

Open hands move in circular movements, simultaneously upwards/ apart, or brush palm to palm, up and down against each other.

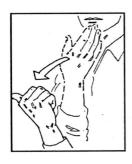

PLEASE, IF YOU PLEASE

Fingertips of flat hand touch mouth, then hand moves down/forward as fingers close onto palm. Can be made without final closing movement.

PLEASED, GLAD, HAPPY

Flat hand rubs in circles on chest, or hands brush together twice, palm to palm (also **enjoy**, **happy**). **Face/body show positive expression**.

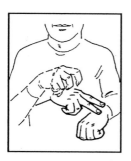

POLICE, POLICE OFFICER

Extended fingers of R. 'V' hand flex as tips are drawn across back of L. wrist.

POOR, ROTTEN, RUBBISH

Edge of R. little finger rubs in small anticlockwise circles on L. palm (also **awful**, **horrible**, **shoddy**). **Face/body show negative expression**.

POSITIVE, PLUS

Extended index fingers are held together at right angles to form a cross. Tap together twice for *positive*.

POST OFFICE, BANK

R. fist stamps palm, then fingers of L. hand. Single contact gives *bank*, and one version of *benefit*, *dole*, *endorse/ment*, *passport*.

PREFER, PREFERENCE

R. closed hand with thumb out, taps L. palm twice (also *acceptable*, *good enough*), or side of thumb taps front of chin twice. **May vary.**

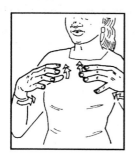

PREPARE/D, GET READY

Thumb tips of palm down
open hands brush
upwards twice on chest,
or tap into chest twice.
Also means *already*.
One hand may be used.

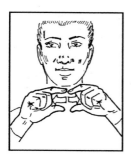

PRIEST, CLERGY, VICAR

Two 'C' hands pull apart
in front of the neck in
outline shape of clerical
collar. One hand may be
used, also a **regional**
sign for *Preston*.

PRIVATE, IN CONFIDENCE

Index edge of flat hand
taps mouth twice, or flat
hands, R. behind L., make
small alternate side to side
movements, in front of
mouth, or other **variation**.

PROGRAMME (TV), FILM

Palm forward R. open
hand rests on L. index
and makes small side to
side shaking movements.
Both hands may move
down throughout.

PUB, PUBLIC HOUSE, BAR

R. fist pulls down/back
twice above left forearm
held across body, (can be
R. hand only). Can be R.
full 'C' resting on L. palm,
or moving to mouth.

PUT OFF, POSTPONE

'O' hands, palm down,
move forward in small arc
(also *defer*, *delay*).
Hands move in backward
arc towards body, for
bring forward (in time).

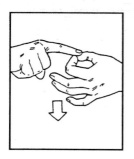

QUALIFICATION/S

Hands form fingerspelt 'Q' formation and make short downward movement. Also means *qualify*, *qualified*, and also *quality*.

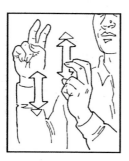

QUARREL, ARGUE

Palm facing bent 'V' hands move up and down alternately, twice, or same movement with indexes pointing towards each other (also *conflict*).

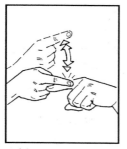

QUICK, BE QUICK, EARLY

Extended R. index finger bounces sharply up off L. index, once, or repeatedly as in *fast*, *hurry up*. Also means *emergency*, *sudden*, *urgent*.

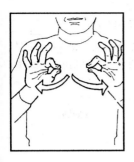

QUIET, BE QUIET, PEACE

Tips of 'O' hands contact then move apart/down (may start crossed). Can start with index on lips pressed together, or with 'Sh' lip-pattern.

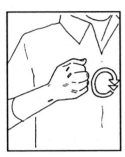

RAILWAY, STATION, TRAIN

Palm left R. closed hand makes several small forward circular movements. Single firm forward movement for *go by train*.

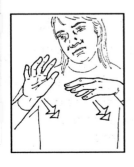

RAIN, RAINING, DOWNPOUR

Open hands make repeated movement down simultaneously. Firm movement down/left with puffed out cheeks for *heavy rain*, *downpour*.

105

READ, SCAN

R. 'V' hand 'scans' across L. palm (fingers represent eye gaze), or in manner to suit **context**, or flat hands palm up/back (*book*) move side to side near face.

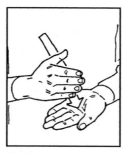

READY, ALREADY

Thumbs of palm down open hand/s tap upper chest twice, (or make upward brushing movements). Also means *get ready*, *prepare/d*.

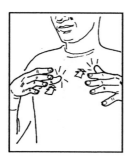

REAL/LY, SURE, TRUE

Edge of R. flat hand hits L. palm, repeated for *actually*, *really*, *surely*, *truly,* or tip of R. extended thumb twists into L. palm (**regional** *real*, *really*).

REASON, BECAUSE, WHY?

Edge of R. extended index finger taps left shoulder, twice. With appropriate **expression for question** form, also means *why?*

REGULAR, ALWAYS, USUAL

R. closed hand, with thumb up, brushes along behind L. palm. R. hand can also be palm back, or palm down on L. Also means *normal*, *ordinary*.

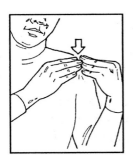

RESPONSIBILITY, DUTY

Fingertips of bent hands move down onto left shoulder ('N' hands may be used). Hands may overlap. Also means *burden*, *depend*, *rely*.

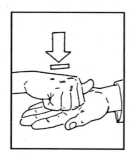

RIGHT, CORRECT, PROPER

R. closed hand with thumb out, bangs L. palm. May contact chest as in *I'm right*, or move and face forward as in *you're right*, and so on, in **context**.

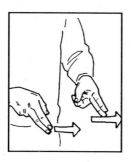

ROAD, STREET, WAY

Two 'N' hands pointing down, twist to point and move forward. Flat hands can also be used. Also means *method*, *path*, *style*, *system*.

ROOM, STUDIO

Extended index fingers point down, (or may point up), and move apart, and then back, in outline shape, or flat hands move in outline shape.

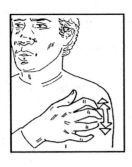

RUDE, BAD-MANNERED

Fingertips of R. clawed hand rub up and down repeatedly on left upper arm (or on side of upper chest). Also means *impolite*, *impudent*.

SAD, DEPRESS, FEEL LOW

Palm down R. flat hand brushes down chest, or in front of nose, palm left (*serious*, *solemn*) or other variation. **Mouth and shoulders droop**.

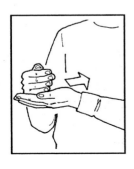

SAFE, RESCUE, SECURE

Edge of R. bent hand rests on L. palm; hands move back to signer, or R. hand brushes back across L. palm. Also means *safety*, *salvage*, *save*, *protect*.

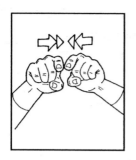

SAME, ALSO, TOO

Extended index fingers pointing forward, tap together twice (or just once), or R. 'N' hand touches nose, then palm up L. 'N' hand (**regional)**.

SCARED, AFRAID, FEAR

Tips of clawed hand tap chest twice as body moves back. Body moves forward with **raised brows** for *really? surprised* (**mouth turns down**).

SCHOOL

Palm forward 'N' hand makes quick side to side downward movement, or palm back flat hand shakes side to side near mouth, or other **variation**.

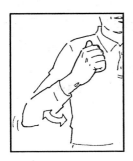

SCOTLAND, SCOTTISH

Elbow makes in and out squeezing movements at side of body.

SHOP, SHOPPING

R. 'Y' hand rubs side to side on L. palm (also means *New York*), or bent hands, palm down, make small downward movements. **Regional**.

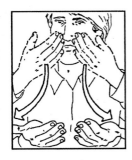

SHOW, DEMONSTRATE

Flat hands held below eyes, palm back, move forward, down and apart. Also means *display*, *exhibit*, *exhibition*, *expose*, *prove*.

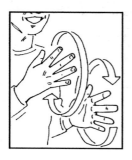

SIGN, SIGN LANGUAGE

Palm facing open hands move in smooth forward circles (may rub together), or twist forwards and back sharply (*chat*), or other changes in **context**.

SISTER

Bent index finger taps nose twice. Bent index on nose flicks straight, or hand makes small downward twist for two **regional variations**.

SLOW, AGES, LONG TIME

Fingers of R. flat hand (or just index finger) move slowly up left forearm, or palm down open hand waves downwards twice (*slowly*, *slow down*).

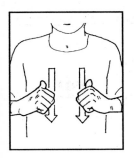

SMART, DRESSY, SUIT

Tips of extended thumbs move down chest. 'Y' hands can be used, or extended fingers of 'N' hand tap side of nose twice (*smart*, *posh*).

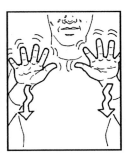

SNOW, SNOWFALL

Palm down open hands, fingers wiggling, move slowly down with small wavy movements, or cupped hands press together (*snow*, *snowball*).

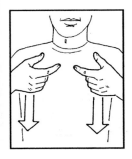

SOCIAL WORKER, WELFARE

Tips of palm back 'C' hands move down chest (also *missioner* now rarely used). Can be repeated. Fingerspelt abbreviation 'SW' also used.

SOFT, EASY, NO PROBLEM

Index finger prods into cheek. Repeat with cheeks puffed for *doddle* etc., or bent hands open and close onto thumbs several times (*soft*, **spongy**).

SOMEONE, ANYONE, WHO?

Upright extended index finger moves in small horizontal circles. A large horizontal circle means *all*, *everyone*. Face/body indicate if **question form**.

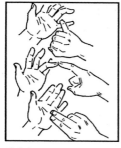

SON

Fingerspell 'SON', or R. index pointing left brushes left across chin, or tips of palm back 'N' hand tap chin, or or other **regional** sign for *boy*.

SPEECH, SPEAK, SPOKEN

Extended fingers of 'N'
(or 'V') hand open and
close onto thumb in short
forward movements, or
index makes small forward
circles near mouth.

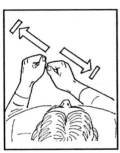

SPORT/S, ATHLETICS

Closed hands move
diagonally apart, twisting
R. to palm up, L. to palm
down, or indexes twist
sharply forward from mouth
or other **regional variations**.

START, BEGIN, COMMENCE

Extended R. thumb
brushes down sharply
behind L. hand, or palm
down open hands snap
shut, twisting sharply to
palm forward.

STAY, BE STILL, REMAIN

Palm down 'C' hands (or one hand) make small firm movement down, or linked bent index fingers move firmly down (also *committed*, *fixed*, *stuck*).

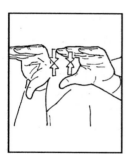

STOP, END, FINISH

Fingers of palm forward bent hands (or one hand) close onto thumbs, or palm forward flat hand is held up, or other **variations in context**.

STRAIGHT, DIRECT, SOBER

Index finger edge of R. flat hand, palm left, touches nose, then hand moves and bends forward from the wrist. **May change in context**.

STRESS, FRUSTRATION

Clawed hands move into chest, one above the other and squeeze shut, twisting inwards against each other (also *grieve*, *mourn*). **May vary**.

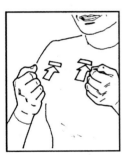

STRONG, ENERGY, POWER

Both fists make short firm backward movement, bending from the elbows, or R. index moves in forward arc down left upper arm (*muscle*).

STUPID, DAFT, IDIOT

Knuckles of closed hand rap against side of forehead twice, or tap against the underside of palm down L. flat hand, or other **variations**.

117

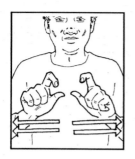

SUBTITLES, CAPTIONS

'C' hands, palm forward, move apart twice, or palm back clawed hand move side to side with fingers wiggling, or **other variations**.

SUMMER, STRANGER

Index edge of bent hand contacts chin, then forehead, or is drawn across forehead to the right (*heat*, *summer*). *Stranger* varies regionally.

SURE, HONEST, TRUE

Edge of R. flat hand hits L. palm with emphasis. Also means *certain*, *definite*, *honestly*, *positive*, *real*. **Open mouth closes with movement**.

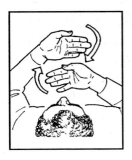

SWAP, EXCHANGE, SWITCH

Palm up flat hands swap places, forward/back or side to side.   May be palm down 'O' or clawed hands, or upright indexes (**people**), and so on to **suit context**.

SWEAR, BLAST, CURSE

Tip of extended little finger moves forward firmly from mouth. **Lips may be pressed together**, or form lip-pattern of various swear-words.

SWEET (taste)

R. index finger twists from palm forward to palm back at side of mouth, or R. thumb tip moves across chin from left to right, or other **variation**.

TABLE, PLATFORM, FLAT

Palm down flat hands start together and move apart. Also means *altar*, *board*, *ground*, *level*, *slab*, and similar meanings.

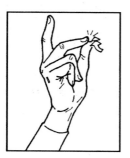

TAXI, CAB

Thumb and middle finger tip click together twice, hand held at head height. **Often fingerspelt**.

TEA, CUPPA

R.'O' hand tips backwards towards mouth, or same movement with closed hand, thumb tucked into bent index. Also means *cafe*, *cup*.

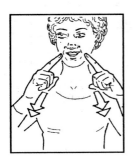

TEACH/ER, INSTRUCT/OR

Index fingers at sides of mouth make two short movements forward, down and apart, or similar movement with bunched hands from temples. **Varies**.

TELEVISION, TELLY, TV

Fingerspell 'TV', or index fingers move apart and down in outline shape, also meaning *monitor*, *screen* or similar items. **May vary**.

THANK YOU, APPRECIATE

Flat hand touches mouth, then swings forward/down, or both hands move from mouth, forward, down and apart. Also means *grateful*, *thank*, *thankful*.

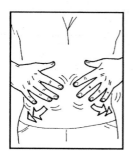

THAT'S ALL, ONLY

Open hands, palm back, shake quickly downwards twice, or palm forward open hands, are held near shoulders. **Shoulders are slightly raised**.

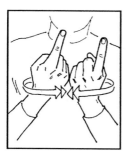

THING, ENTITY, ISSUE

Closed hands with index fingers extended, twist round and tap together twice. May tap repeatedly, moving to the right, also meaning *issues*.

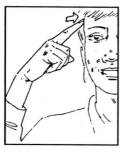

THINK, THOUGHT

Index finger taps forehead (twice for *sensible*, with **eyebrows raised**), or makes small circles, **brows furrowed**, for *imagine, mull over, ponder, presume*.

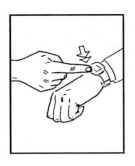

TIME, WHAT TIME?

Tip of R. index finger taps back of L. wrist twice, or fingers of open hand wiggle, or R. index on L. palm wiggles (also **clock**). **Brows raised if question**.

TOILET

R. index of fingerspelt 'T' taps edge of L. hand (or L. palm) twice (also means **Tuesday**), or thumb of 'Y' hand brushes chest twice. **Many variations**.

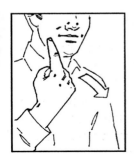

TOMORROW, NEXT DAY

Index finger contacts side of chin, then swings forward/down, to palm up. With middle finger also extended, means **in two days time**.

TRAFFIC LIGHTS

Full 'O' hand held forward with palm facing back, springs open, moves down and repeats twice. Both hands can be used simultaneously.

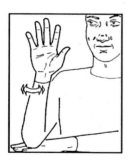

TREE

R. open hand placed with forearm upright on back of L. hand, twists at the wrist several times. Formation moves round in arc for *forest*, *wood*.

TRY, ATTEMPT, EFFORT

R. index finger brushes forward against L. May repeat. Single sharp movement gives *majority*, *most*, *mostly*, and *special*, *very* (**regional**).

TUBE, METRO, SUBWAY

R. index moves under L. bent hand (also *Eurostar, tunnel, underground*). Brushing sharply against L. palm, also means *escape, truant*.

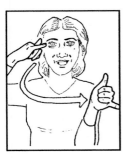

TYPETALK, RELAY CALL

R. 'Y' hand moves forward in arc from ear towards L. 'Y' hand held forward. See *Typetalk* and *TextDirect* details in Useful Contacts, page 144.

UNDERSTAND, IDEA, REALISE

Index finger flexed on thumb at side of forehead, flicks up. Also means *initiative, invent, invention* (with **raised eyebrows**). **May vary.**

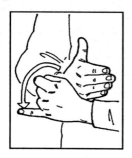

UNTIL, FINALLY

R. flat hand moves forward from left shoulder onto extended L. little finger (also **weekend**), or from right shoulder, to contact palm back L. flat hand.

UPSET, DISTRESSED

Flat hand on chest makes small upward brushing movements. A single slow downward movement gives **calm**, **gentle**, **mild**, **quiet**.

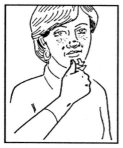

USE, USEFUL

Tip of thumb (or tips of bent hand) brushes down chin twice. Index tip on cheek moves forward/ down as hand springs open for **used to**, **au fait**.

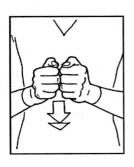

VALUE, VALUABLE, WORTH

Closed hands held together make two short downward movements. Bunched hands can also be used. Also means *precious*.

VARIETY, RANGE, VARIOUS

Index fingers move up and down alternately, moving to the right, or moving apart. Also means *assorted*, *etc*, *kinds*, *sorts*, *varied*. **Varies.**

VIDEO, VCR, RECORDER

'V' hands, palm down, move in horizontal circles. Palm up open hands drop down closing to bunched hands for *video copy*, *record*, *taped*.

127

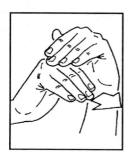

VISIT, ENTER, GO IN

R. bent hand moves forward under L. hand or turns and moves back to signer (**directional**). Can be 'V' hand prodding side of neck or other **variation**.

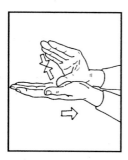

WAGES, PAY, SALARY

R. bent hand with thumb on L palm; fingers close onto thumb as hands move back to body. R. hand may be clawed and close as hands move back.

WAIT, HANG ON

Bent hands (or closed hands) palm down, move down slightly, twice, or flat hand is held up. As shown is also a **regional** sign for *shop*, *shopping*, *London*.

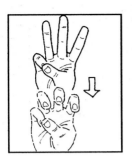

WALES, WELSH

Hand held palm forward with index, middle and ring fingers extended and open. Hand makes small movement down as fingers bend.

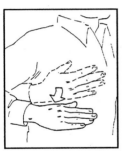

WANT, NEED, WISH

Flat hand on side of body, makes small movement down, twisting to palm down. Also one version of *desire*, *hope*.

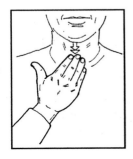

WATER, THIRSTY

Fingertips of bent hand brush down throat, twice, or thumb tip of 'Y' hand, or 'O' hand brush forward twice on cheek or other **variations**.

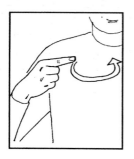

WE, US

Index finger makes forward arc from one side of chest to the other. Handshape may vary to incorporate number of people referred to, or other **variations**.

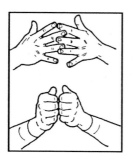

WEEKEND

Both hands form brief fingerspelt 'W', pull slightly apart, and close together, or R. hand moves down left arm onto L. little finger. **Regional**.

WHAT? WHAT FOR?

Extended index finger, palm forward, shakes in short quick side to side movements. **Face/body show question form**.

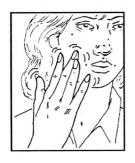

WHEN? WHAT TIME?

Open hand held at side of cheek with fingers wiggling. **Face and body indicate question form**.

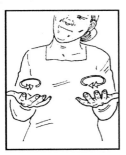

WHERE? WHEREABOUTS?

Palm up open hands (or one hand) move in small inward circular movements, or move in/out towards each other. **Face/body indicate question form**.

WHICH? EITHER, BETWEEN

Palm down 'Y' hand moves side to side or between items or people referred to. **Directional. Face and body indicate if question form**.

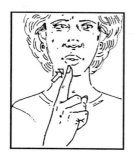

WHO?

Palm left R. index (or bent index) taps chin twice, or thumb of 'L' hand on chin, index flexes. **Regional. Lips are rounded, face/body show question form.**

WILL, WOULD, SHALL

Closed hand twists from palm forward to palm down on cheek (also *after*, **regional**), or same movement with extended index fingertip on cheek.

WIN, ACHIEVE, SUCCEED

Palm left R. clawed hand snatches closed, sharply moving to the left across L. palm. Can be R. hand only at head height, or other **variation**.

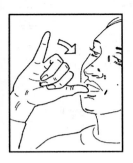

WINE

Thumb of 'Y' hand touches mouth as hand tips backwards. Held straight with small tapping of thumb on chin means *pipe*, *smoke a pipe*.

WITH, TOGETHER

Index, middle finger and thumb of L. hand close onto extended fingers of R. 'N' hand. Hands may move forward (*go with*, *accompany*). **May vary**.

WOMAN

Side of index finger brushes forward twice on cheek. Also means *girl* *female*, *feminine*, and is a **regional** sign for *always*. **May vary**.

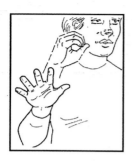

WON'T, WOULDN'T, REFUSE

Fingers flexed behind thumb spring open as hand moves sharply forward from side of chin. **The head shakes**.

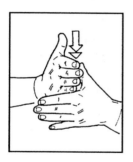

WORK, JOB, CAREER

Edge of R. flat hand chops down twice onto index edge of L. flat hand, at right angles. A small sawing action gives a regional sign for *wood*.

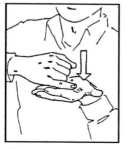

WRONG, EVIL, FAULT, SIN

Edge of R. little finger taps L. palm twice. With **raised eyebrows** means *what's wrong/the matter?* On chest means *I'm wrong, guilty*. **Directional**.

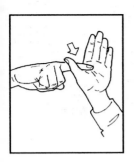

YEAR

R. index finger moves down to form fingerspelt 'Y'. May make single brushing movement down. Repeat for regional signs for *yellow*, *young*.

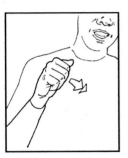

YES

Closed hand twists to palm down, in nodding movement, as **the head nods**. R. hand can rest across L. index. Can be palm back (**directional**).

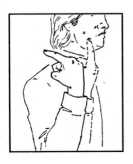

YESTERDAY, DAY BEFORE

Index finger, palm back on cheek, drops back/down, or moves to point back over shoulder. Middle finger also extended means *two days ago*.

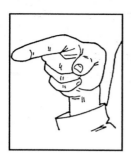

YOU

Index finger points and makes short movement towards person referred to. Hand sweeps round in small horizontal arc for plural.

YOUR, HER, HIS, ITS

Closed hand, palm forward, moves slightly forward, or towards person referred to, accompanied by **eyegaze** (also *your/her own* etc).

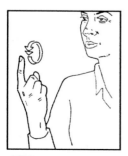

YOURSELF, PERSONAL/LY

Upright index finger, palm back, makes small forward circles directed towards referent, accompanied by **eyegaze**. Also means *herself*, *himself*, *itself*.

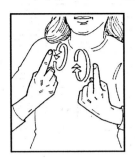

YOURSELVES, THEMSELVES

Upright index fingers,
palm back, make repeated
alternate forward circles
directed towards
referents, **accompanied
by eyegaze**.

ZIP, ZIPPER

Tips of index and thumbs
of both hands touch, then
R. hand moves up and
down. Location and
direction **may vary in
context**.

ABOUT FINGERSPELLING

Fingerspelling is a manual representation of the letters of the alphabet, and although it is an important and integrated part of BSL it relies on the understanding of English (not the first language of most born deaf people) and its use varies considerably between individuals.

Drawings give a static image of the alphabet, but in fluent use, the shapes can merge and appear quite different, so that they are recognised as word patterns, and this requires practice. Words can be spelt out in full, abbreviated or initialised.

Fingerspelling is commonly used for names and places. Days of the week and months of the year are also often a repeated initial or abbreviated pattern, e.g. *Wednesday* - 'WW', *January* - 'JAN', and so on.

See pages 16-17 for Left and Right-Handed versions of the British Fingerspelling Alphabet.

Manual Alphabet for Deafblind People

As illustrated, the R. hand represents the sender forming the letters onto the passive L. hand of the deafblind person.

AMERICAN ONE-HANDED FINGERSPELLING ALPHABET

SOURCES/RECOMMENDED READING

British Deaf Association (1992). *Dictionary of British Sign Language/English.*
London: Faber and Faber.

Pinker, S. (1994). *The Language Instinct.*
London: Penguin Books Ltd.

Smith, C. (1996). *Sign Language Companion: A Handbook of British Signs.*
London: Souvenir Press.

LET'S SIGN: *BSL Building Blocks* Teaching Resources: Co-Sign Communications.

Taster Pack
(Tutor with CD-Rom, and Student Primer)
Full colour A2 BSL Greetings Signs and Fingerspelling Wallchart
Set of A4 Poster/Mats:
Greetings-Family-Feelings-Questions
A4 Bildtafeln zur Deutschen Gebärdensprache:
Tätigkeiten - Familie - Fragen - Gefühle

LET'S SIGN: *Early Years*

LET'S SIGN: *For Work*

Available from libraries, bookshops and by mailorder from Forest Bookshop (details overleaf).

USEFUL CONTACTS

Numbers for voice contact are indicated by (V)
and for text contact by (T)

British Deaf Association (BDA)
1-3 Worship Street, London EC2A 2AB.
Tel: 020 7588 3520
Textphone: 020 7588 3529
Fax: 020 7588 3527
Helpline Textphone: 0207 588 3529 (V/T)
Helpline Textphone: 0800 652 2965
Helpline Telephone: 0870 770 3300
e-mail: helpline@bda.org.uk   **web:** www.bda.org.uk

Centre for Deaf Studies
University of Bristol, 8 Woodland Road,
Bristol, Avon BS8 1TN.
Tel: 0117 954 6900 (V) 0117 954 6920 (T)
Fax: 0117 954 6921
Videophone: 0117 9706253
web: www.bris.ac.uk/deaf

**Council for the Advancement of
Communication with Deaf People (CACDP)**
Durham University Science Park, Block 4, Stockton
Road, Durham DH1 3UZ.
Tel: 0191 383 1155 (V/T) **Text:** 0191 383 7915
Fax: 0191 383 7914
e-mail: durham@cacdp.org.uk
web: www.cacdp.org.uk

Deaf Studies: University of Central Lancashire
Preston PR1 2HE.
Tel. +44 (0)1772 892400 [V]
Tel. +44 (0)1772 893104 (text)
Deaf Studies Team Fax: 01772 892966
e-mail: cenquiries@uclan.ac.uk
web:www.uclan.ac.uk

Deaf Studies: University of Wolverhampton
School of Humanities, Languages and Social Sciences
University of Wolverhampton
Wulfruna Street
Wolverhampton
WV1 1SB.
Switchboard: 01902 321000 (Abroad: +44 1902)
Fax: 01902 322739
e-mail: K.Dekesel@wlv.ac.uk
Web: www.wlv.ac.uk/sles

The Forest Bookshop Warehouse
(Specialists in Books, Videos,
CD-Roms on sign language/deaf issues)
Unit 2 The New Building, Ellwood Road, Milkwall,
Coleford, Gloucestershire. GL16 7LE
Tel: 01594 833858 (V/T)
Videophone: 01594 810637
Fax: 01594 833446
e-mail: Forest@forestbooks.com
Web shopping site: www.ForestBooks.com

The National Deaf Children's Society (NDCS)
National Office 15 Dufferin Street, London EC1Y 8UR.
Tel: 020 7490 8656 (V/T)
Freephone Helpline:
Mon-Fri 10 am - 5 pm 0808 800 8880 (V/T)
Fax: 020 7251 5020
e-mail: helpline@ndcs.org.uk   **web:** www.ndcs.org.uk

The Royal National Institute for Deaf People (RNID)
19-23 Featherstone Street, London, EC1Y 8SL.
Tel: 020 7296 8000 (V) 020 7296 8001 (T)
Fax: 020 7296 8199
Informationline: Tel: 0808 808 0123 (freephone)
Textphone: 0808 808 9000 (freephone)
e-mail: informationline@rnid.org.uk

web: www.rnid.org.uk

TYPETALK: National Telephone Relay Service
Helpline 0800 500 888 (text) 0800 7311 888 (voice)
0151 709 8119 (fax)
BT TextDirect.
Users can dial directly to the person they want to
speak to.
Text users dial **18001;** Voice users **18002;**
then the area code and number wanted.
In emergencies, textphone users can dial **18000 (no
other number needed)**.
This number alone connects a call to the emergency
services and a Typetalk Operator will join the line to
help relay the call.
e-mail: helpline@rnid-typetalk.org.uk
web: www.typetalk.org